EXPLORING THE STATES

Massachusetts

THE BAY STATE

by Amy Rechner

BLASTOFF!
5
READERS

Note to Librarians, Teachers, and Parents:

Blastoff! Readers are carefully developed by literacy experts and combine standards-based content with developmentally appropriate text.

Level 1 provides the most support through repetition of high-frequency words, light text, predictable sentence patterns, and strong visual support.

Level 2 offers early readers a bit more challenge through varied simple sentences, increased text load, and less repetition of high-frequency words.

Level 3 advances early-fluent readers toward fluency through increased text and concept load, less reliance on visuals, longer sentences, and more literary language.

Level 4 builds reading stamina by providing more text per page, increased use of punctuation, greater variation in sentence patterns, and increasingly challenging vocabulary.

Level 5 encourages children to move from "learning to read" to "reading to learn" by providing even more text, varied writing styles, and less familiar topics.

Whichever book is right for your reader, Blastoff! Readers are the perfect books to build confidence and encourage a love of reading that will last a lifetime!

This edition first published in 2014 by Bellwether Media, Inc.

No part of this publication may be reproduced in whole or in part without written permission of the publisher. For information regarding permission, write to Bellwether Media, Inc., Attention: Permissions Department, 5357 Penn Avenue South, Minneapolis, MN 55419.

Library of Congress Cataloging-in-Publication Data

Rechner, Amy.
 Massachusetts / by Amy Rechner.
    pages cm. – (Blastoff! readers. Exploring the states)
 Includes bibliographical references and index.
 Summary: "Developed by literacy experts for students in grades three through seven, this book introduces young readers to the geography and culture of Massachusetts"–Provided by publisher.
 ISBN 978-1-62617-020-9 (hardcover : alk. paper)
 1. Massachusetts–Juvenile literature. I. Title.
 F64.3.R43 2014
 974.4–dc23
                                                                        2013002421

Printed in the United States of America, North Mankato, MN.

Table of Contents

Where Is Massachusetts?

Vermont

New York

Massachusetts

Worcester •

Springfield •

Connecticut

Rhode Island →

Massachusetts is a **New England** state. Its eastern coast juts into the Atlantic Ocean. It is shaped like an arm showing its muscle. New York is the state's western neighbor. To the north are New Hampshire and Vermont. Connecticut and Rhode Island lie to the south.

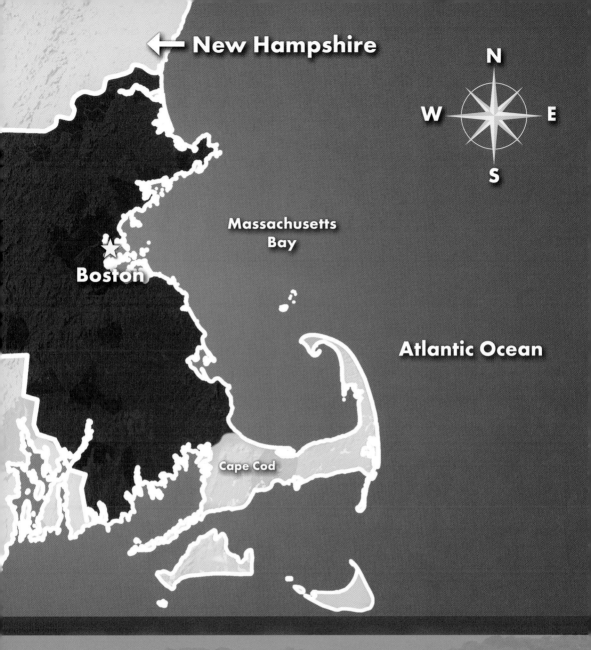

New Hampshire

N
W   E
S

Massachusetts
Bay

Boston

Atlantic Ocean

Cape Cod

Massachusetts is one of the country's smallest states. From the western border to the ocean, it is only 183 miles (295 kilometers) across. The capital city of Boston sits on a harbor in Massachusetts Bay. The shape of the bay protects Boston from strong ocean winds and waves.

History

Native Americans came to Massachusetts more than 10,000 years ago. In 1620, the Pilgrims arrived from England on the *Mayflower* ship. They were the first European settlers in the area. They started Plymouth **Colony**. More English settlers soon followed. In 1775, the first shots of the **Revolutionary War** were fired at Lexington and Concord. Massachusetts became the sixth state in 1788.

Mayflower

Massachusetts Timeline!

1620: The Pilgrims arrive in Massachusetts. They settle at Plymouth after a month on Cape Cod.

1692: Three young Salem girls accuse townspeople of witchcraft. The Salem Witch Trials begin. Nineteen people are found guilty of witchcraft.

1770: British soldiers kill five colonists in the Boston Massacre.

1773: Colonists object to a British tea tax. A group dumps tea from a ship into Boston Harbor. This becomes known as the Boston Tea Party.

1775: The "shot heard 'round the world" starts the Revolutionary War. Colonists fight the British Army in the Battles of Lexington and Concord.

1788: Massachusetts becomes the sixth state.

1797: Massachusetts native John Adams becomes the second President of the United States.

1876: Alexander Graham Bell invents the telephone in Boston.

1960: Massachusetts native John F. Kennedy is elected the thirty-fifth President of the United States.

Boston Massacre

Salem Witch Trials

Boston Tea Party

The Land

Massachusetts has more than 1,500 miles (2,400 kilometers) of ocean shoreline. The land is rocky and sandy in the east. Streams and rivers cut through **fertile** farmland in central Massachusetts. Small lakes and ponds dot the region. The Mount Holyoke mountain range looms over the Connecticut River Valley.

Western Massachusetts is home to the Berkshire Hills and Taconic Mountains. There, woodlands provide shelter for wildlife. The state's highest point is Mount Greylock in the northwest corner. It stands 3,491 feet (1,064 meters) tall. Massachusetts' weather ranges from cold, snowy winters to warm summers. Fierce winter storms called "nor'easters" batter the coast.

fun fact

The largest lake in the state is the Quabbin Reservoir. It was built in the 1930s to provide drinking water for Boston and other communities.

Quabbin Reservoir

Berkshire Hills

Massachusetts' Climate
average °F

spring
Low: 38°
High: 56°

summer
Low: 61°
High: 79°

fall
Low: 44°
High: 60°

winter
Low: 22°
High: 37°

Cape Cod

Cape Cod National Seashore

Cape Cod covers the hook-shaped **peninsula** southeast of Boston. Off its southern coast are two large islands, Martha's Vineyard and Nantucket. The Cape is home to cranberry **bogs**, rock and sand beaches, and forests. Much of its Atlantic shore is a protected area called Cape Cod National Seashore.

Did you know?
The island of Nantucket was once the whaling capital of the world. The whales caught by Nantucket ships were used for meat and oil.

Brant Point Lighthouse
Nantucket Island

Cape Cod draws many visitors every year. Small seaside villages line the peninsula all the way to the tip. Lighthouses dot the coast. People enjoy hiking the many nature trails and watching for whales and seals. Shell collecting is another favorite activity on Cape Cod's beaches.

Wildlife

Massachusetts is home to a wide range of wildlife. Bobcats and black bears prowl the western part of the state. Moose can be seen in central Massachusetts. Woods and wetlands provide habitats for deer, foxes, and beavers.

Massachusetts' woodlands shelter woodpeckers and swallows. Bright scarlet tanagers are found in old forests. Ducks, geese, and swans nest near the rivers. The saltwater bays around Cape Cod are home to loons. Humpback and fin whales swim off the coast.

black bear

scarlet tanager

Atlantic puffin

fun fact

Nor'easters bring more than bad winter weather to Massachusetts. A rare bird called the Atlantic puffin is sometimes sighted along the coast in stormy weather.

bobcat

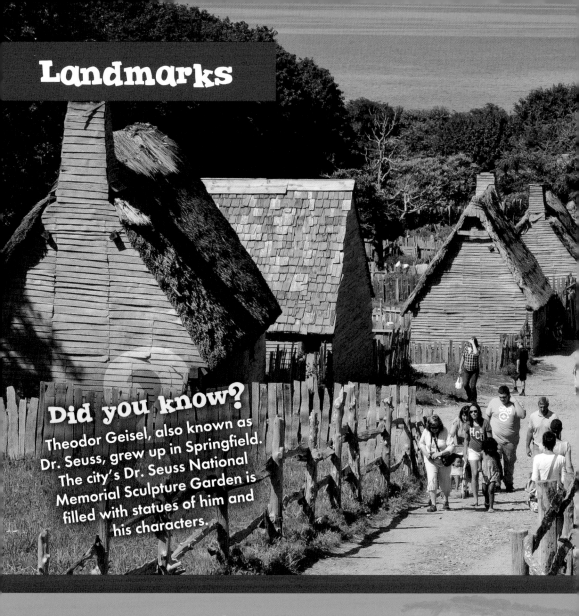

Did you know?

Theodor Geisel, also known as Dr. Seuss, grew up in Springfield. The city's Dr. Seuss National Memorial Sculpture Garden is filled with statues of him and his characters.

The past comes alive in Massachusetts. At Plimoth **Plantation**, costumed actors show how people lived in the original Plymouth Colony. Salem's Witch House is one of many sites that mark the spooky witch **trials**. Many people visit the home of President John Adams and his family. It is now part of Adams National Historical Park in Quincy.

Plimoth Plantation

New Bedford Whaling Museum

Higgins Armory Museum

fun fact

The Higgins Armory Museum in Worcester has one of the world's largest collections of weapons and armor. It includes a Roman gladiator helmet, samurai swords, and Viking weapons.

Old Sturbridge Village near Worcester showcases New England life in the early 1800s. Whaling is the focus at the New Bedford Whaling Museum. A different kind of sea life is on display at Fall River's Battleship Cove. It is a **maritime** museum with the world's largest collection of U.S. Navy ships.

Boston

Boston is one of the country's oldest cities. Much of its history has been preserved. The Freedom Trail offers a walking tour of historic sites. These include the Paul Revere House, Old North Church, and the USS *Constitution*. Nearby, Faneuil Hall Marketplace is a small historic area filled with shops and restaurants.

People come from around the world to live in Boston. They work at banks, hospitals, and technology companies. Others are students at the city's many colleges and universities. Boston is a special blend of American history and international culture.

USS *Constitution*

Working

Did you know?

Massachusetts is the nation's second-largest producer of cranberries after Wisconsin.

Massachusetts is small but mighty. Factory workers make equipment such as computers and electronics. Scientists conduct research in medicine and technology. Many of the state's workers have **service jobs**, especially in **tourism**. The state's beaches and historic sites draw visitors from around the world.

Along the coast, fishing boats bring in tuna, lobster, and scallops. Their catches are sold in grocery stores and restaurants. Workers dig gravel and sand from the coast's rocky soils. Farmers in central Massachusetts raise dairy cows. They also grow cranberries, apples, and other crops.

Where People Work in Massachusetts

manufacturing
7%

farming and
natural resources
1%

government
11%

services
81%

Playing

The fun is outdoors in Massachusetts. The Atlantic coast draws swimmers, sunbathers, and sailors in the summer. Downhill and cross-country skiing bring snow lovers west to the mountains. Hikers enjoy miles of trails through the state's forests in all seasons. Fall's changing leaves attract visitors to the Berkshire Hills.

Basketball was invented in Springfield in 1891. Now the Boston Celtics are an NBA success. Boston's Fenway Park is a historic baseball park. The Red Sox who play there have some of the most loyal fans in the country. Bruins hockey and New England Patriots football also keep sports fans busy.

fun fact

More than 20,000 people run the Boston Marathon each year. Started in 1897, it is the world's oldest marathon.

Fenway Park

Boston Cream Pie Cupcakes

Ingredients:

- 1 package (2 layer size) yellow cake mix
- 1 package (3.4 ounces) instant vanilla pudding mix
- 1 cup cold milk
- 1 1/2 cups thawed Cool Whip, divided
- 1 package (4 ounces) semi-sweet baking chocolate

Directions:

1. Heat oven to 350°F.

2. Make cake batter and bake as directed on package for 24 cupcakes. Cool completely.

3. Beat pudding mix and milk with whisk for 2 minutes. Let stand 5 minutes. Use serrated knife to cut cupcakes horizontally in half. Whisk 1/2 cup Cool Whip into pudding mixture. Spoon onto bottom halves of cupcakes, using about 1 tablespoon for each. Cover with cupcake tops.

4. Microwave remaining Cool Whip and chocolate in small bowl on high for about 1 1/2 minutes. Stir after 1 minute. Chocolate should be almost melted. Stir until blended. Let stand 15 minutes. Spread onto cupcakes. Refrigerate 15 minutes.

baked beans

Did you know?
Boston is nicknamed Beantown because of its famous baked beans recipe.

oysters

clam chowder

Early settlers in Massachusetts relied on simple dishes such as baked beans and corn pudding. **Game** birds, cranberries, and orchard fruits were plentiful. Seafood such as cod, oysters, and clams has always been popular. New England clam chowder is a famous soup. Visitors to Cape Cod enjoy clambakes and lobster boils.

Massachusetts also has a sweet tooth. Marshmallow Fluff spread was created in the state. The Toll House chocolate chip cookie was developed at a small Massachusetts inn. The official state dessert, Boston cream pie, isn't a pie at all. It is a layer cake with custard filling and chocolate frosting.

Festivals

Massachusetts packs a lot of fun between its borders. On Patriots' Day, people relive the Battles of Lexington and Concord at Minute Man National Historical Park. Springfield hosts The Big E, New England's state fair. Its Avenue of States features a **replica** of each original New England state **capitol**.

Music lovers enjoy outdoor concerts at the Tanglewood Music Festival in the Berkshire Hills. The Boston Pops Orchestra presents a Fourth of July concert with fireworks along the Charles River. Small festivals celebrate the harvest and changing fall colors across the state.

Minute Man National Historical Park

Boston Pops
Orchestra

John Adams

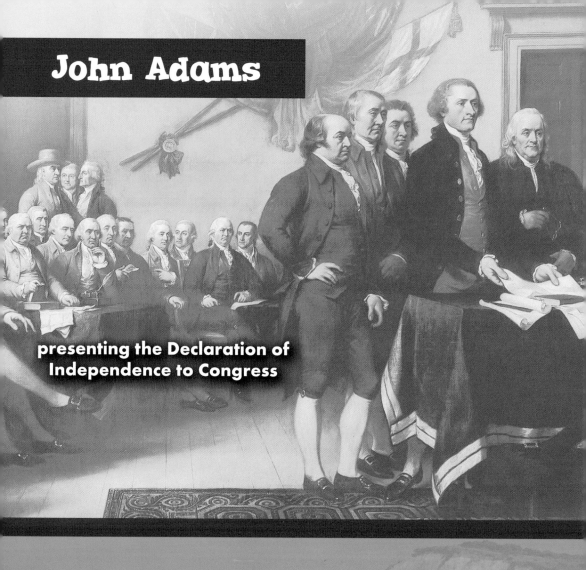

presenting the Declaration of Independence to Congress

John Adams helped write the story of American independence. The Massachusetts native began his career as a Boston lawyer. In 1770, he defended British soldiers in court after the Boston **Massacre**. Adams believed everyone deserved a fair trial. At the same time, he wanted American independence from the British. In 1776, Adams helped Thomas Jefferson write the Declaration of Independence.

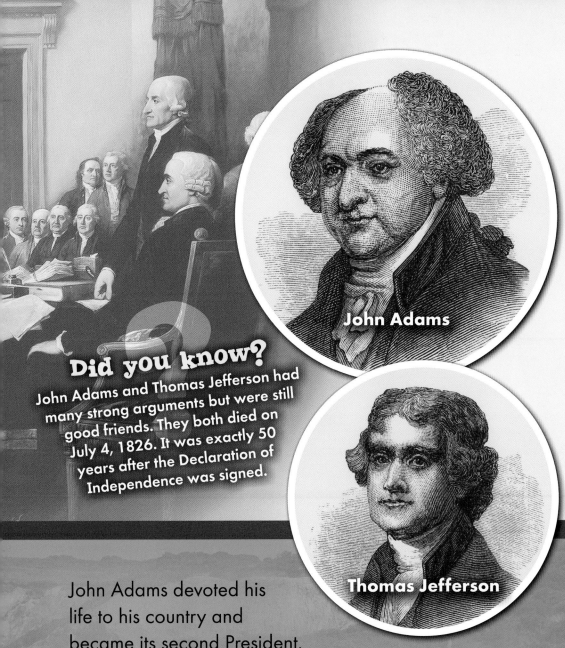

John Adams

Thomas Jefferson

Did you know?
John Adams and Thomas Jefferson had many strong arguments but were still good friends. They both died on July 4, 1826. It was exactly 50 years after the Declaration of Independence was signed.

John Adams devoted his life to his country and became its second President.

Adams' love for his home state remained strong through many years away from his Quincy farm. He was proud to be from Massachusetts. He was even more proud of the new nation he had helped to create.

Fast Facts About Massachusetts

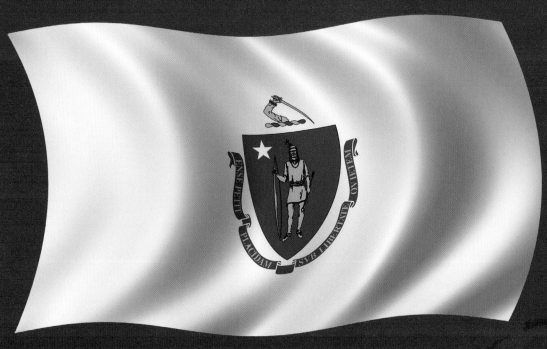

Massachusetts' Flag

The Massachusetts flag is white with the state seal in the center. The blue and gold seal shows a Native American making a sign of peace. The silver star in the upper left shows the state was one of the thirteen original colonies. An arm and sword and the state motto surround the blue shield.

State Flower
mayflower

State Nickname:	The Bay State
State Motto:	*Ense Petit Placidam Sub Libertate Quietum*; "By the Sword We Seek Peace, but Peace Only Under Liberty"
Year of Statehood:	1788
Capital City:	Boston
Other Major Cities:	Worcester, Springfield
Population:	6,547,629 (2010)
Area:	8,262 square miles (21,398 square kilometers); Massachusetts is the 44th largest state.
Major Industries:	manufacturing, fishing, services, tourism
Natural Resources:	fish, timber, gravel, sand, rock
State Government:	160 representatives; 40 senators
Federal Government:	9 representatives; 2 senators
Electoral Votes:	11

State Bird
black-capped chickadee

State Animal
right whale

Glossary

bogs—areas of wet, spongy ground

cape—a point of land that extends into the sea

capitol—the building in which state representatives and senators meet

colony—a territory owned and settled by people from another country

fertile—able to support growth

game—wild animals hunted for sport or food

maritime—relating to the sea

massacre—the violent killing of many people

native—originally from a specific place

New England—a group of six states that make up the northeastern corner of the United States

peninsula—a section of land that extends out from a larger piece of land and is almost completely surrounded by water

plantation—a large farm that grows coffee, cotton, rubber, or other crops; plantations are mainly found in warm climates.

replica—an exact copy of something

Revolutionary War—the war between 1775 and 1783 in which the United States fought for independence from Great Britain

service jobs—jobs that perform tasks for people or businesses

tourism—the business of providing services to travelers

trials—events in which citizens are questioned and judged in a court of law

To Learn More

AT THE LIBRARY

Jerome, Kate Boehm. *Boston and the State of Massachusetts: Cool Stuff Every Kid Should Know.* Charleston, S.C.: Arcadia Kids Pub., 2011.

Jurmain, Suzanne. *Worst of Friends: Thomas Jefferson, John Adams, and the True Story of an American Feud.* New York, N.Y.: Dutton Children's Books, 2011.

Trueit, Trudi Strain. *Massachusetts.* New York, N.Y.: Children's Press, 2008.

ON THE WEB

Learning more about Massachusetts is as easy as 1, 2, 3.

1. Go to www.factsurfer.com.

2. Enter "Massachusetts" into the search box.

3. Click the "Surf" button and you will see a list of related Web sites.

With factsurfer.com, finding more information is just a click away.

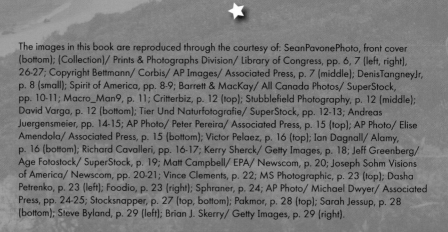

Index

The images in this book are reproduced through the courtesy of: SeanPavonePhoto, front cover (bottom); (Collection)/ Prints & Photographs Division/ Library of Congress, pp. 6, 7 (left, right), 26-27; Copyright Bettmann/ Corbis/ AP Images/ Associated Press, p. 7 (middle); DenisTangneyJr, p. 8 (small); Spirit of America, pp. 8-9; Barrett & MacKay/ All Canada Photos/ SuperStock, pp. 10-11; Macro_Man9, p. 11; Critterbiz, p. 12 (top); Stubblefield Photography, p. 12 (middle); David Varga, p. 12 (bottom); Tier Und Naturfotografie/ SuperStock, pp. 12-13; Andreas Juergensmeier, pp. 14-15; AP Photo/ Peter Pereira/ Associated Press, p. 15 (top); AP Photo/ Elise Amendola/ Associated Press, p. 15 (bottom); Victor Pelaez, p. 16 (top); Ian Dagnall/ Alamy, p. 16 (bottom); Richard Cavalleri, pp. 16-17; Kerry Sherck/ Getty Images, p. 18; Jeff Greenberg/ Age Fotostock/ SuperStock, p. 19; Matt Campbell/ EPA/ Newscom, p. 20; Joseph Sohm Visions of America/ Newscom, pp. 20-21; Vince Clements, p. 22; MS Photographic, p. 23 (top); Dasha Petrenko, p. 23 (left); Foodio, p. 23 (right); Sphraner, p. 24; AP Photo/ Michael Dwyer/ Associated Press, pp. 24-25; Stocksnapper, p. 27 (top, bottom); Pakmor, p. 28 (top); Sarah Jessup, p. 28 (bottom); Steve Byland, p. 29 (left); Brian J. Skerry/ Getty Images, p. 29 (right).